SICKTOWNE.

PEOPLES ART COVENANT – P.A.C.

By Casimir Chotkowski, M.S. Ed., M.S., S.B.L
and Alemapyk Sodoh

Books by Casimir Chotkowski, M.S. Ed., M.S., S.B.L and Alemapyk Sodoh.

Available on Kindle e books and Amazon.

The Sicktowne series, PG-13.

Sicktowne. Money Tree. The story of a town growing into a city. An innocent lady caught in a web of corruption. A decent man discovering deceit.

Sicktowne. People's Art Covenant P.A.C. Political maneuverings in a small town.

The Bully Survival Guide series, PG-13.

Available on Kindle e books and Amazon.

Bully Survival Guide. Vol. 1. Beat Down Individual Stand UP!

Bully Survival Guide. Vol. 2. Bully Neighborhood.

Bully Survival Guide. Vol. 3. How to Survive Bully.

Foreward

The Sicktowne series of books are works of fiction. Any resemblance to persons living or dead is pure coincidence. I dedicate the books to my children. They have always been sturdy and strong. I love and admire all of them.

Chapter 1

The Rainmaker

The Rainmaker sat in the small back corner office sifting through the files that contained millions of dollars—all printed on 8.5 x 11 inch pages. He was trying to decide which Corporations could be pushed into his name and which could be left in the name of Lady Jane Winslow. The Rainmaker knew her, and liked her and the only thing she ever shared with him was her nickname for the town, she called it "Sicktowne –with an e." She added, I spell it with an 'e' at the end "because the town's real name ends in an 'e'." It stuck in his head like that. The Advisor had gone off to cry himself a river over her death and the Rainmaker felt that if he was going to be left to clean up the mess he should take whatever he wanted. The Advisor didn't know the ins and outs of the corporate filing system. The Rainmaker knew he could do anything he wanted to and the Advisor would sign off on it. He decided to treat himself to one big fat company, one medium money maker and one small fry just to cover all of the aggravation he was going to go through to change the dates on everything and to transfer the titles from Lady Jane to her daughter, also Lady Jane. That would leave an even dozen for him to split with the Advisor. If the Advisor noticed, the Rainmaker knew that by the end of the year he would have at least three more giants in the group anyway. Next year the Advisor would be the Mayor and the Rainmaker would be sitting here figuring things out alone unless he could get one of the guys from the Peoples Art Covenant to help him. He was on the board of "The Covenant," the Artists group that was pushing all the money into town from Manhattan. He knew his buddy Arty would come in and give him a hand. All he had to do was ask. Arty ran the Peoples Art Covenant Gallery and was the go to guy for all the information about the money in the "Covenant" organization. By this time next year the "Covenant" project would be spewing out money like an ATM. The Rainmaker was already pushing the money it was generating now into his own off shore accounts. It was going to be fun to watch the town turn into "East Manhattan," and to realize that just 60 miles from the big apple they had created an Artistic Empire. The local folks never knew what hit them. The Advisor and his Trustees had stepped in quietly and moved buildings around like a monopoly board game. The new Art House was built specifically to hold up "The Covenant" and to upset the colloquial mentality that had dragged the town down for years. He enjoyed it. His Father had owned a stylish clothing store on Jane Street for 30 years, when he passed, the local Chamber of Commerce voted the space to another merchant. The Rainmaker resented losing what he considered to be his birthright. He vowed that in his lifetime he would find a way to usurp the power of the local Chamber and build a company that would control *them*. Six years ago he did just that when he started the Peoples Art Covenant, P.A.C. as in pack your bags and go. That's what he had planned for the Chamber and any of the members who were still alive who had voted his Fathers space away. "The Covenant" as the insiders called it had grown with a membership of more than 1500 people from all areas of industry. There weren't that many Artists in the area so anyone could join. Dues were twenty bucks a year. This year they would be able to produce a Music "Festival on the Lake" that would headline some pretty big name acts and would generate over 100 thousand dollars in revenue for other projects. Most of that money would go to the Art House to promote the marketing for the Manhattan Artists while paying off the local merchants. The

merchants were promised a bump up in sales when
they supported the Art House, the Rainmaker knew
that was never gonna happen. Nobody bought any
Art in Sicktowne, they didn't' have that kind of
disposable income and they hated the thought of
the loose ended Bohemian lifestyle. They were
suspicious of Art in general. He created a slush
fund for the merchants, he told them that they
could split whatever the Covenant Artists who
lived in the Art House made. The merchants were
clueless, the Covenant Artists never made *any*
money in Sicktowne, all the money came from
Manhattan. Most of the local families couldn't
fathom what was going on behind the scenes
either. If they knew they would fight it anyway.
They had organized a group to try and stop the
construction of the new Linen Building. A luxury,
6 floor condominium that was just being finished.
They didn't want it to be built in town, their
reason-- they thought there wouldn't be enough
parking to accommodate the town! He laughed out

loud as he remembered that meeting. Three hundred idiots trying to block progress because they would have to walk an extra 100 feet to eat at a restaurant! He almost couldn't believe it. The Trustees paid out for the permits and went around them. Then they used the sign in sheet from the meeting to locate the main organizers and messed with them until they lost their jobs. They drove the organizers houses into foreclosure and messed with their kids. Eventually, broke and almost homeless, 30 of them had showed up to apply for a low income apartment in the Linen Building. When they moved in, the Trustees planned to break them down until they all went homeless. They would know that nobody would help them. The local Police were paid out of the slush fund. The courts were too. It always ended the same way, they wound up homeless or dead. He was done for today and he patiently organized all the files and put them in his briefcase. He looked around the small office to be sure that he didn't forget anything, shut off the lights and closed the door. As he headed down the steep stairwell he realized that it was getting close to dinner time. The office was a free space for any of the Trustees to use whenever they were in town. It was tucked away on the second floor of the Sicktowne Library. The Library was housed in an old former Woolworth building in the heart of town. He had his choice of restaurants for dinner and he knew that it didn't matter which one he chose to go to, someone he knew would be there. Everyone in town knew him. He could eat in any restaurant for free. They were all serving his wines. His real passion was wine and he was part owner of an east end Vineyard. The bar and restaurant owners knew that if they planned to do business in Sicktowne, all the wine sales would have to go through his company. He stepped out into the milieu on Jane Street and headed across the street. The #1 restaurant in town was already filling up and he saw 2 friends who waved him over.

11

Chapter 2

"Mail Terrorist"

She was listening to "I believe in Miracles," the funk sound from the 70's as she put the finishing touches on the phony postal registration mark that would deliver her latest masterpiece for free. She was deciding which one to use. She tried to keep them in order. No one paid for postage anymore— why would you when you could just borrow one that belongs to a massive corporation. They don't keep track! She was juggling the "mail stalking" of three people this month. A big job if you consider how many pieces of mail she had to create each day. Five a day was the minimum that each account paid for and they were always late with the "stalking information" that she needed to make the advertisements fit the victim. It wasn't easy. Sometimes she was up until midnight waiting for a caller to check in and give her the correct information to help her design a psychologically damaging ad that had to be in the victims mailbox the very next day. Then she had to be out by 8:30 a. m for the early postal deliveries, to hand off the mail to the right carrier for delivery with all the regular mail. She couldn't miss the regular delivery or she would have to wait until the next day and the "mental punch" didn't have the same effect when it was a day late. The game was that these victims had to know that they were being followed every single day. Skipping a day gave them a break to catch their breath and that was unacceptable in the business of a "Mail terrorist." The stalkers who hired her wanted their victims to feel the pain every day. They had to be pushed to the breaking point. They needed to die and they better kill themselves, that way no insurance company would lose money on a life insurance payout. She was surprised at how much her business had increased as the economy dropped. People were getting really mean. She finished her last piece of mail for the day and put them all in her sachel as the radio played 110th Street by Bobby Womack. "How appropriate," she thought, my job is to put pressure on people. The song haunted her as she moved around her studio to shut off her computer, printer and copy machine. The stack of logos still needed to be filed and the folder with the assorted post marks was askew on her drawing table. She had most of them scanned in to use but some of them need to be cleaned up. She might get to that tomorrow. One of her customers was finishing up at the end of the week. Usually someone would hire her to "terrorize" a victim for six months at a time. Most people usually got the idea by then, but some of them were thick or slow and they needed another 3 to 6 months of terror to wake up to what they needed to do. If a guy wasn't paying his taxes and he was living in one of "The Covenant" houses, she would send him 5 advertisements and letters referring to taxes *in the same day*. She'd keep going with the tax theme until someone from the Town offices called her and cleared his name off the list when he paid his taxes. Sooner or later even the slower ones got the message. It could be any message, from anyone about anything. As long as they paid her she would design any kind of psychologically appropriate mail that they wanted. Her most recent campaign of terror was against a lady who decided to try and open a free Art gallery down in Sicktowne. "The Covenant" was not going to let that happen and they pummeled her for over a year with mail and surveillance. They messed with her oldest daughter, her mortgage and even stole her identity. The lady was so freaked out that she not only closed the gallery, she vacated her house and moved away. It was no surprise to any of the Artists that the U.S. Post Office was bleeding out. Nobody had to pay for postage anymore; for every corporation that paid for one postal registration, three companies "borrowed" the registration to send their mail for free. The fat corporations never found out about it and if they did, it would take so much leg work to find the thieves that it wasn't worth it. She would save any of the new non-profit registrations that came in her mail and sometimes sign up for mail from other non-profit organizations to get new ones.

Chapter 3

Gallery of fools

The old "school Marm" sat alone addressing
envelopes for the next Artists reception. She
thoroughly enjoyed her volunteer activities at the
Peoples Art Covenant Gallery. She had retired 12
years ago from her teaching position at Sicktowne
High School. Her 30 year pension paid out at more
than 110 thousand dollars per year and her home in
the first class section of town was paid off. Her
husband was an investment Banker in Manhattan
and her passion was Art. She was buying up as
much of it as she could this year. After supporting
the Peoples Art Covenant for the past 5 years, she
was finally getting the inside track for purchasing
the most collectible Art. The Sicktowne Teachers
Organization – "T.O" was counting on her to
invest their money wisely. They wanted to make
money off of the Art. They had increased their
Real Estate holdings when the local and national

housing market went bust. She was always working with the Realtors in the town to move a poor family out of a foreclosure and into one of the new low income units that were being created to get the poor and unconnected families into the "off island loop." Every year the school districts combed through the Teachers lists of really poor families to decide who would be moved "off island." It kept the area from being inundated by the homeless who eventually became mentally ill or fell into drugs, gambling or prostitution. Life went slower and easier in the South and it was easier on the poor. Long Island was a dog eat dog environment because it cost so much money to live on it. Most of it was already "owned off." The ancient families had the best real estate and companies. They kept the foundation of the towns running. The schools were the second largest employers and they weeded out the have nots. The businesses would support whoever graduated and the colleges would cull from the smartest and wealthiest to ensure that they remained at their higher standard of living. The larger and older the family name, the more power they controlled. The smaller poorer families were manipulated into leaving or they were just worked to death in low end jobs and eventually killed off. The lagging economy just couldn't support so much dead weight anymore. Someone had to decide who would eat and who wouldn't; and who better to decide? The Town Elders had decided that the Teachers were with the kids every day and they knew everything about them and their families. They kept "the records." The old "family books" were kept in small back offices in each school building. Teachers could make entries into each "Family Log" when a new child was born, when a family member died. It all came out in the classroom. Eventually everything moved into the computer system, now, there were websites that helped them manage the history of every family tree. There were no secrets on an island that was only 20 miles wide and 120 miles long. The ancient families realized that they had to play ball with the others to survive. Over the years they had developed a plan for survival. Two or three elders would agree to intermarry their families to create a super family. They wouldn't marry outside of their circle. Each town had its own inner circle where everyone just knew that the Jolitte family always married the Wampolo's and always would. It had been going on for years. Each member of the family was placed in a plum position in a corresponding school district, county job, railroad position, or replaced a retiring family member in a job that they were holding down. The system insured that the haves always "had" and the "have nots" never prospered. The school Marm was born into an ancient family so she got her school district job and now represented the Art investment branch of the local Teachers Organization, "The T.O." Other members represented other arms of investment and she was thrilled to work for the

Arts. She was a retired Reading teacher and she always said that if certification had been required in her generation she would have been an Art teacher. Instead, she finished her four year degree off island and came back to walk into a job vacated by her Uncle. She still had many contacts with past students in the town and those students helped her when she needed "special" contributions. Her classroom was special and she was able to choose her own students from among the best families. Everything had changed now but there were still classrooms and Teachers who were designated as "A List," and reserved for the best families. A poor kid could get in but only if they socialized and became best friends with an "A List" student; usually before the second grade. After that the kids kept strictly to the "Haves Only" schedule and socialized only within that group. The "School Marm" was almost done with her stack of letters and the afternoon sun was streaming onto the paintings and changing them from their "day colors to night colors" she thought to herself. As she paused to look out at the parking lot she saw Arty coming towards the building. "Here comes the Hippie," she said under her breath. "We'll see what corrupt plan he has for the organization today," She heard the door open and looked up, Arty immediately stopped to admire a painting and without looking at her said, "How's it going Rose?" in his most dry voice. "I'm fine Arty, how are you?" she answered in the same plain tone. "We've got to talk about the mailing. I've got another registered postmark to use. Seems like someone snitched to the Postmasters Office in Washington! Can you believe it? They figured out that the local office is corrupt, went past our friends at the state level and got all the way up to Washington! The U.S. Post Office is bleeding out anyway, it's like a free for all out there, everyone is using everyone else's registered postage and now this. Let's just switch it over, better safe than sorry," he finished. "Just in time for this batch," she called to him as she waved the stack of envelopes in the air. "I was just about to attach the old postmark to them." Arty stepped into the small office at the back of the gallery and handed Rose the U.S. registered postage mark to copy. As she began copying the stamp onto each envelope he walked to the painting hanging just outside the office. "Has anyone been in today?" he asked. Rose answered in her coldish voice "We had the past Director of the local Museum come by. She left her card. She was wearing the most outrageous mink vest! She is as corrupt as they get around these parts, her husband was running this County some years ago and she got the Museum job as a handoff from another Bureaucrats wife. Anyway, she stopped in and made herself known. She didn't say what she wanted. She just left her card." "I've met her socially and she's a snob, "Arty said dryly." The locals hate her and her Museum because they know that she takes their tax dollars and spends them all in Manhattan." Arty replied. It never occurs to them that there aren't any quality Artists living in their town or in the whole county for that matter. Not many really." "That is where we disagree Arty!" the "school Marm" Rose snipped. She hated that elitist attitude and all of the Manhattan folks had it. "An Artist is not defined by his or her location. The truly talented will create beautiful work no matter where they live or work. It flows through their veins and oozes from their pores. They've got antennae you know. They see things we can't see and feel things we don't feel. Manhattan Artists are no different than Long Island Artists." "Yes, my dear, Artie patiently responded "but I'm referring to the quantity of Artists, not the *quality*. You always seem to misunderstand me here. Strictly by the numbers, there are more Artists to choose from in Manhattan because there are many more people there—and Artists are *people*" "Alright Arty, alright already, I'm not going to go over and over this every time I see you. We agree on the quantity, we disagree about the quality." Rose had slipped on her jacket and marched out the door. Arty was staring at the business card that she had handed to him " The Isit Art Museum, Director" He made a copy of the card on the office copy machine and he wrote, 'add to mailing list,' across the top and left the copy on the office desk, he put the card in his wallet and sat at the sign in table. He could smell the scent of Rose all over the cushioned folding chair and he crinkled his nose in disgust. He didn't have to wonder why she never taught at college level, she was an idiot. He had never taught in the public schools because he was stone cold drunk for the first 40 years of his life. He tempered it with weed. At 42 he had recovered from a near death experience with the bottle and now at 46 he was coming into his own. He had known plenty of 'Roses' over the years and was even married to one in his twenties but that type of lady was long gone from his world now. That was the kind of woman who had held him back for so many years.

Constantly misunderstanding his work, his life, his laissez faire lifestyle. He hated those uptight, obsessive compulsive head hunters. "She'll stroke herself out in a few years," he found himself thinking. "Those types never know how to relax." He found himself pursing his lips as if to draw in on a cigarette, but was wishing for a joint instead. "Not going down that path again old boy," he chided himself, "one thing leads to the other," and the spin from the Peoples Art Covenant was just hitting and he was having a wonderful time. "Not going to screw this up as the money is just taking off for me." He was sick and tired of living in poverty and he knew that was changing every single day now. His long brown hair fell over his eyes as he started to read through the sign in sheet for the most recent opening reception to see if any of his friends' names were on it. He chuckled to himself, as he wound his hair into a loose pony tail. Another reception with twenty people in attendance. That's why he always thought of it as a "gallery of fools." Planted in "east Bumpkinville," the gallery was a showplace for the local community, it was a "front" for the Art House. The Advisor had promised to deliver Art to the local community and Arty was responsible for culling from the local redneck Artists' to mix in a few Manhattanites and present something palatable to everyone. He wondered how he did it without drinking.

Chapter 4

Here comes the Bride

Mickey never really recovered from losing Lady
and as the months went by he missed her more and
more. He still went to the annual events that they
always shared and even more now that he was the
new "Advisor" with a new Mayor and a few new
Trustees. It was all right but it would have been a
heck of a lot more fun if Lady was there to share it
with him. Instead, he felt like his constant
companion was the Mayor and he was a total drag
since he lost his "one true love," his Lady. He had
sobbed like a baby on Mickey's shoulder the day
she died and Mickey on his. It was hard to relive.
At the funeral he had to comfort Lady's daughter,
"Baby Lady" and that almost made him lose his
mind. Lady had mailed him a kind of 'suicide
note' to let him know that he was Baby Lady's real
Father. He had kept the note and its contents to
himself. Talk about a painful twist. He was

writing in emotional pain through the whole thing. He never told Baby Lady anything, why add to the churn at this painful time? There would be plenty of time later on to tell her in his own time. He remembered staring at her birth certificate that morning. Like everyone else, he thought her name was exactly like her Mothers; Lady Jane Winslow—but it wasn't. Baby Lady's name was Lady Jaden Winslow, just like his family name, Michael Jaden. He never got a chance to ask Lady anything and he imagined many conversations that he would have liked to have had with her. "Death is so permanent" he thought out loud. "Yes it is dear," Emerald responded as she sat down on the plush, confederate grey chenille sofa next to him. He was pretending to watch Golf on the huge flat screen television in their family room. She placed a tray of mini garlic knots on the square coffee table, the marinara sauce spilling slightly out of a blue glass bowl. "Yum!" he stated. He was so sick of "finger foods" but he wouldn't dare complain.

Emerald was his new bride and at 18, she could
hardly be expected to create a full course dinner
every night. She was at the beginning stages of
cooking, he thought, for the first three months she
had perfected her salads. Now she was going into
breads and "finger foods." He figured her next step
would be soups. "You're a wonderful cook my
bride!" he chirped as he grabbed for the ball of
carbohydrate. "Heart attack on a plate," his Mother
would have said. He dipped it into the watery
marinara sauce and popped it into his mouth. He
had learned to smile and eat anything. "We're
coming into our nine month anniversary" she
beamed at him with a toothy white smile. "I know
my sweet, I love you my pookie," he breathed as
he slid over to give her a big bear hug. They fell
back onto the sofa kissing. She giggled, "My boo!"
he gave her side a tickle and sat back up. The golf
was ending and she knew his favorite investigative
journalist show was coming on next. "I'm gonna
order out for dinner," she told him. "Do you have a

preference?" She knew he wouldn't care, as long as she figured out the meals, he would eat it. He had made very clear to her that in their relationship he was going to be "the boy" and she needed to be "the girl," in the most old fashioned of ways. He did not want to run the house or be in the kitchen and he would never touch a vacuum. She could have a household budget, hire a cleaning service and even have part time help in the kitchen if she wanted it. He would handle all the money and anything that had to do with the cars and outside landscaping and the family investments and it would really please him to have his dinner on the table every night around 6pm. He didn't believe that this was too much to ask. She was going to have a privileged life, a vacation to a warm place in the Winter and another to a cool place in the Summer. She would accompany him to the events of the season wearing the most fashionable clothing and meet the most interesting people. She must maintain a proper level of physical attractiveness for her own sake and for his success at work. He had just accepted the position of "Mayors Advisor" and he had to present a wholesome appearance. Emerald was excited for her new role as his wife and she was happy with the life that was being presented to her. The thing that she missed most about graduating from High School into "Wife School" was the one thing that wasn't on the schedule-- having some fun. Her friends wouldn't come over on a Sunday evening to watch a news show, they were all out in her old High School group eating appetizers at the local Sports Bar. She was distracting herself from the drudgery of the past 9 months by preparing the finger foods they would be eating at the bar. She would order the same things for dinner that her friends were texting to her describing what they were having for dinner at the local teenage friendly restaurant. Sometimes she joined them on a Saturday night if there wasn't an award dinner at the local catering hall. She would drink too much and flirt with her old High School boyfriend. Spring Break had been particularly painful when her friends came back from college and wanted to go out all night, every night till the early morning hours. Mickey was wonderful about it, but she wound up feeling more depressed. She had asked her Father for part time work at his car dealership and he let her come down to "Reds Car dealership" whenever she liked. She had spent most of her childhood running through the car lot so it was her home away from home. Now, she spent most of her afternoons hanging out with the salesmen in the showroom. She could meet young people when they came in to look at the shiny new cars and her High School friends could hang out with her without having to be so serious with "Mickey Mouse" as they called him, her new husband. She was wise beyond her years after watching her Father haggle and maneuver deals with the biggest organizations in town. She knew Mickey was head over heels in love with her and that he couldn't help being 45. She also knew that by this time next year he would want to start planning for a baby and she wasn't sure if she wanted to trade her youth for that new responsibility. She kept her own conscience about it all because her High School friends weren't interested in babies and she'd be pregnant during the semester they would be traveling through Europe. She knew better than to mention a word of it to her Mother. Emerald knew that in her excitement for a Grandchild, her Mother would just blow things up to an unbearable situation and Lady would feel even more pressure to have a baby.

Chapter 5

The Mayor

He still wasn't used to having people call him
"The Mayor." It was his childhood dream and he
had given up on it years ago. Now as he plotted his
retirement it didn't matter all that much to him. It
had its share of excitements, but none of them ever
made him forget about Lady. She was his for just 6
years but the memories would be his for a lifetime.
He ached for her to see him as Mayor. He was
never able to release the feeling of sadness that had
been dwelling within him from the moment that he
had heard that Lady was gone. It lived in him
every day. People who had known him for years
noticed the lag in his smile, they thought he would
be effervescent as Mayor, and he would have been
if he had his Lady with him. They'd say "you'll
shake it off give it some time." He agreed while
presenting his biggest Mayoral smile. At her
funeral, the Mayor had to stand with his friends

and watch as community members streamed through. Like many men and especially Politicians, he had learned to push his feelings down so deeply that he could smile while on fire if he had to. This was the same kind of feeling; he was being emotionally flayed. Finally, he had a few moments with Lady to try to absorb her beauty into his soul. His heart was crushed as he knelt at her casket, the senseless end of her still young life was like a black hole in his mind. He knew why she chose to go and he knew she had to go. He just couldn't cope with the loneliness that had fallen upon him. Last year when they were at the local Cable Station preparing to shoot a public service announcement, Lady had told the crew that she really didn't' know anybody and she didn't have any family around her. The cable company owned the biggest newspaper on the Island and the crew had decided that Lady would be a great "story." They put a team of writers together to bring a scandal to her and her daughter. No authorities would help her as the story was being "developed" which was "newspeak" that referred to how they scheduled the surveillance and stalking that they brought to her doorstep. No Therapist or Lawyer would be available to counsel her about the painful situations that would be perpetrated against her. She would know that she was alone. The Mayor shook his head from side to side at her casket and he didn't hold back as the tears rolled down his cheeks. The beautiful and delicate pink and yellow flowers on the bodice of her dress brought back many memories of sunny days with her. He would have done anything for her but the machine that was coming against her was too huge for him to do anything about, he just had to stand by and watch her weather the personal storm. She had perished in it, anyone would have. He felt a small relief to know that she had gotten away before they were able to make her watch them ruin her daughter. The boyfriend that they had sent for Baby Lady was a demon from hell. The Mayor remembered

the boy and his family from years ago when he
was a school Principal. They were the most
criminal ridden family in the County. He never
knew if Lady was aware of who the boy was. She
never mentioned it. He only knew that she was
heartbroken at losing her daughter. The Mayor had
made her daughter know how much she had hurt
her Mother. The girl was wrapped in stony silence
as she sat with Lady's closest friend, Mickey. She
wore a mask of trauma for the two day wake and
she finally broke down in hysteria as they closed
the casket. She looked just like Lady from twenty-
five years ago. "So beautiful," he thought. She
could have had any guy she chose, instead she was
unwittingly sitting with the animal that had been
chosen for her. The Mayor didn't wait for closing
speeches, he was driven to the cemetery and he sat
in his limousine, alone until the procession arrived
to bring his Lady to the plot he had chosen for her.
She wouldn't be alone, he had purchased a double
gravesite, in the event that her daughter would

need one as well. He had his own family plot to go to eventually, but he felt that the thought of being with Lady might linger in him and as the years went by, if the desire didn't quell, he wanted to be sure that she was not lying next to a stranger.

Chapter 6

The Penthouse

Without Lady, The Mayor didn't want the Penthouse anymore. It was decorated for her taste and for his life with her. Now, he didn't know how to get rid of it. He was in Manhattan for his monthly Art meeting and he had invited a large part of the party crowd back to the Penthouse. This evenings meeting was to address the need for more Manhattan Art at the Long Island college campuses. The colleges wanted to build portfolios and cash was too hard to manage in a swindlers market and too hard to hide. Art was the 'new' stronger investment. There was nothing new about the Art market, but it was new to the Sicktowne community. The Sicktowne Chamber of Commerce had wooed a large college to the area 25 years ago and another smaller college just 15 years ago. They were convinced that Sicktowne would be stronger as a "college town." The Mayor had pushed for new buildings and the Arts. The colleges wanted investments and he was involved in bringing them. Paintings were pretty but Sculpture, and outdoor Sculpture in particular was the money maker now. The colleges went for it. Their campuses were the last open tracts of land in the county. The construction industry was collapsing and it was anticipated that every available piece of land would be built upon within the next 10 years. There wouldn't be any more new home building projects. The small town Main Streets and highways still had open land but they were being reserved for office buildings and apartment houses. Everything was already owned by one of the ancient families. Further East, was still being developed but with each new storm, more land was being washed away and fewer and fewer people were interested in waterfront property on an island that was beginning to sink. The oldest college in the area had hired a slightly autistic bi-polar Sculptor to teach a class part time.

She was connected to the Manhattan Art crowd and they gave her enough money to begin to fill their "Big West" campus with Manhattan Sculpture. The largest Sicktowne College was envious and they put out the word to the Peoples Art Covenant, simply stating "We Want World Class Art." The Covenant aimed to deliver. The Mayor was thrilled. The local Sicktowne Artists who were born and raised in the area were led to believe that if they supported the building of and moved into the Art House, they would be able to make a living as an Artist. When the money started funneling in the locals were moved out and the Manhattan Artists were moved in. As generations of their families had done before them the local Artists were forced to stand and watch the money come from and go back to Manhattan. To be a "local" Artist was the kiss of death in their own town. The one local Artist who had tried to open a gallery in her own town had been summarily rejected by the Covenant and driven from the town and her home by ruthless methods of torment. No other Artist would dare to try to touch the Sicktowne Art industry. The Mayor was relieved to see the number of Artists who had come back to the Penthouse party. He was looking for his own contact to bring Sculpture to the large and small college campuses in Sicktowne. Arty did all right but he was still a burnt out Hippie with limited resources. He was hoping that the Sculptor who controlled the "Big West" college Art would team up with him. Everyone called her "Big West." He was watching her as she stood with a plate full of green olives, working a toothpick to pull the red pimiento from the green holes. She was convinced that eating olives would help her lose weight. The red pimiento pieces were meticulously arranged all around the edge of the plate like a slimy fence to keep the olives from rolling off. Her autistic tendency kept her from making regular eye contact with anyone and the "olive project" was giving her something to focus on. Every so often she would dip into her jacket pocket and pull out something that looked like Parsley to sprinkle on top of the olives. As the Mayor approached he could see that it wasn't Parsley, it was pot. He sidled up to her and asked, "How are the olives this evening?" "Big West" replied, "Well, I'm definitely a green olive lover and these really aren't too bad." She speared a pot covered orb with her beige wooden toothpick and held it up to the Mayors mouth. "No, thank you," he waved her hand away, "Salt gives me terrible heartburn, and I've got enough aggravation to begin with." Big West laughed and said "I hear ya, and a lot of mine is standing right in this room." He asked her "Is it worth the trouble to deal with these types of personalities? I've been thinking about putting together a collection for my large Sicktowne campus. Do you think you could work with my guy to put something together?" Lady's moniker for the town had caught on like wild fire. After what they had done to her daughter, she had taken the time to tell everyone she saw at every community event, "call it Sicktowne, everyone does," and now everyone did. Big West raised her eyebrows with delight. "That sounds interesting to me. Call me on Tuesday morning at the campus gallery, we can talk about things." The Mayor felt a surge of happiness for the first time since he lost Lady. One of the crowd danced over to Big West and pulled her toward the middle of the room where other characters were dancing to loud party music. He always called them characters because they were the strangest people he ever met. This group was an average bunch. Freezing cold weather with snow on the ground and many of them were wearing flip flops, he didn't understand it. He looked down at his oxfords and realized that he was on the other end of the spectrum of creativity.

Chapter 7

Mickey the Lawyer

Baby Lady was ready to go as Mickey pulled up to her Mothers' house. She had moved back home two months after her Mothers' funeral. Her boyfriend was standing with her, his hood pulled deep over his eyes. She looked so young and beautiful, so much like her Mother. His heart pounded as he saw her pouty mouth and high cheekbones. It was the first time that he realized that she looked like many of the women in his family as well. "She's my daughter," he thought to himself incredulously. She waved as she saw him and gave him the little girl smile he had come to know. "Come on in my pretty girl," he called out as she pulled the car door open. The boyfriend hauled himself into the back seat of the Buggatti. "Man this is outrageous!" he shouted. "Sit tight, Alan. This rides for Lady." Mickey shot back to shut the boyfriend down. "He's excited to be in the car Uncle Mickey!" Baby Lady told him. She had placed her hand on his right arm and squeezed. "You ready for this Baby?" Mickey asked. "I guess so," she answered, "Mom was so beat down at the end. She didn't have any money, she was in that house and people were making her miserable. Now, I have the house, and I have Alan there with me. The neighbors have been very kind to me. What was happening to my Mother? Did she tell you anything? I found boxes full of mail in the basement, she had them in clear zip locked bags with the date of each delivery. What was that about? I found her financial papers for the house and the car and she didn't have much else as far as I can tell, so I'm thinking today is just going to be a follow-up to nothing." Mickey turned right onto "Accident Alley" and headed down towards Sicktowne. A local Lawyer friend of his had helped Lady over the years. He was a good guy, but he was deeply involved with the political machine that ran the town and he was good friends

with the Mayor. They pulled up to the office and
Alan who was silent for the ride over yelled out,
"hey this is a Psychotherapy Office!" He pointed
to the big wooden sign out front. "And the sign
below it says "Law Office" doesn't it? Mickey said
flippantly. He hated the kid and he was planning to
find Lady a decent guy when this whole thing blew
over. Alan didn't have a job and he wasn't going
to get one in Sicktowne. Mickey would see to that.
Mickey was in the Department of Labor "chain of
friends" and a member of the oldest organization
in town. They knew how to get rid of riff raff like
Alan. He helped Baby up the steps and he could
see through the large glass window in the door that
no one else was in the office. Alan was lagging
behind, still staring at the "Psychotherapy" sign.
He was remembering something that one of his
friends had told him about the office and as he was
about to step up to the first wooden planked
staircase he shouted out, "You two go on in, this is
family business. I'm going across the road to the

gas station to hang out with my buddy." He turned and began to sprint away from them. Mickey slammed the door behind them, glad to be rid of the trash. Baby started to cry. She knew Alan was going to ditch out, he always bolted when the going got tough. She was grateful to have Uncle Mickey to cling to. She was overwhelmed as if her Mother had just passed again today. The wound re-opened by the finality of dealing with her last will and testament. The Lawyer shook her hand and led them to the small conference room. Blue damask overstuffed chairs with deep brown everywhere else made Baby feel safe. The Lawyer went over the deed for her house and had her sign off on ownership. He showed her a small six thousand dollar life insurance policy and had her sign for permission to allow him to contact the agency to collect the death benefit. Then he looked at Mickey and asked "Did Lady have any other investments? Corporate or otherwise? That you know of?" Mickey shook his head and shrugged

49

his shoulders, he replied "You know who her *friend* was, she could have been doing something with his group." "Everyone knows who her *friend* was Uncle Mickey—the new Mayor, let's not pretend anymore." Baby demanded. "Ok, as long as we're all on the same page, let's look at her credit reports. It's not standard but I always order them when there's a potential suicide. They reveal the most interesting things about people. This is Lady's." He spread the sheets out on the conference table. "Tell me, how is it that she is listed as 'owner' on 15 Corporations? She's a multi-millionaire on paper. Yet her savings and checking accounts are almost empty and her house is in foreclosure. Have you ever heard of her mentioning any of this?" Mickey and Baby were speechless. "This isn't anything I've ever heard from Lady. This can only be one group. Is Baby going to inherit this money?" Mickey asked. "I don't know," stated the Lawyer. "I'm going to have to report this as fraud to the Attorney General and I really don't want to have anything to do with it. I can see where it's going and it could end with me losing my friends, my family and my practice in this town. I want to sign off on it. I also will give you the credit report for Baby and hers is now identical to Lady's so somebody is doing some creative financing somewhere. It's too big for me Mickey, I want out." Mickey couldn't believe what he was hearing from his old friend. He guffawed nervously in disbelief and said, "You gotta be kiddin me right buddy? Who made Lady the "fall guy" and why would they need to get Baby involved?" The Lawyer was gathering up the papers and he stood as he picked up the folder and held it in front of Mickey. He moved to open the conference room door and said, "I don't know anything about this, you will have to find someone else to work on this with you." He indicated with an outward motion of his hand that Mickey and Baby needed to leave his office. They gathered their jackets and as they left, Mickey reached over

to shake the Lawyers hand and say "Thank you."
Baby echoed him and they stepped out to the car
bewildered. Alan could see them come out through
the large plate glass windows that surrounded the
cashier at the gas station. His buddy was telling
him about the group that controlled the camera that
was aimed at the Lawyers front door. The group
had formed to keep an eye on the "Psychos" who
went into the office for treatment. They would
follow them home and alert their neighbors. They
felt that they were doing a community service by
letting people know that they had a "looney" in
their neighborhood. His buddy at the gas station
called them the "Loon Crew." Alan was sweating
at the thought of it. He was glad that he had
dodged that bullet. He watched as Mickey drove
Baby away in the black Buggatti. He knew that
Baby had seen him and she was crying as her
Uncle Mickey turned left onto "Accident Alley.
Alan knew he would meet her at her house later
on. He knew that she was alone. Once he got her

away from her Mother, she had no one. Baby was starting out as Lady had ended up-- alone with no family around her. "Uncle Mickey" had been a surprise to him. No worries, what he couldn't do, "the group" that had followed them down the road would finish. He was considering a move back to one of his ex-girlfriends. Life with the "Loon Crew" following you couldn't be pretty and Baby would have to figure this one out for herself he thought. Baby had always understood, she'd say the same thing each time he disappeared, "Men take care of themselves first, then they consider others. Women take care of others first and meet their own needs last." He knew she was right.

Chapter 8

Lady Jaden

Mickey pulled over to side of "Accident Alley" to pick up a pizza as Baby sat sobbing in the car. "It'll be fine Baby. We can figure things out," he said as he put the box into the back seat. He put the 2 liter soda on the floor by Baby's feet. The drive back to Kingdom Lake was silent. At her house, Baby opened the front door and Mickey looked up and down the street to see if any neighbors were watching. A silent silver car slid past the stop sign and turned left onto Trolley Boulevard. They stepped into the living room. The tiny house was covered in clothing that had been left for someone else to pick up. Baby gathered up the pieces that were strung along the back of the sofa and placed them on top of the small dining room table. She cleared off magazines and papers from the coffee table and Mickey placed the pizza box in the center. Baby brought two cups, plates and napkins from the kitchen and they sat together on the sofa. The house seemed be unnaturally quiet as they began to eat the lunch. Neither one wanted to speak but conversation was the only way to keep the spirit of Lady alive. Mickey couldn't think of an easy way to open the topic of his Fatherhood to Baby so he tried to sound casual as he asked her " Have you heard from your Dad?" Baby shook her head and said "uh uh" through her mouthful of pizza. "Do you keep in touch with him?" Mickey continued. "Not really, Mom hated him so I just gave up trying to know him when I was about 12. He never tried to reach out to me so I just kinda figured he didn't care." Mickey methodically folded his pizza in half to finish the first piece. He took a deep breath and said quietly, "Well Baby, just before your Mom passed she told me that I'm your Father." Baby jolted with the shock of hearing him say it out loud. She had suspected that he was her Father years ago, but her Mother would never let her talk about her feelings. "Oh my goodness Uncle Mickey, I know. I guess I've always known." She felt a sense of relief and comfort to finally feel that she belonged with someone. Losing her Mother was tragic and she had spent many nights crying. Alan was useless. When she got too overwrought he would leave to go party with his friends. Eventually she pushed every feeling down and was content to walk around feeling numb all of the time. She started to quietly weep. Mickey put his arm around her shoulders and said "It's gonna be okay Baby. You've got nothing to worry about. I'll make sure we get everything straightened out. You know I've loved you all your life." Baby had placed her unfinished pizza on the table and was lying back on the couch cushions. Mickey was stroking her honey colored hair back from her forehead. He was holding her left hand as he faced her. "I'm so thrilled to know that you are my daughter. I'm so happy to have you as my family. You can just keep on calling me Uncle Mickey, I don't know what else to say." Baby was staring at her "Uncle Mickey" and wondering what his whole family looked like. The happiness and joyful thoughts of having him for a Dad and having his family as her own were hard to process as she was trying to cope with the pain and loss of losing her Mother. All she could say was "Okay." They finished eating in loud silence, each one chewing over their thoughts in the tiny home. Outside, Alan waited, smoking his cigarette. Baby wasn't answering any of the text messages he had been sending. He could see the black Buggatti and he wanted the Uncle to leave so that he could eat and crash. He had been watching the house for an hour now and he was making a note of the steady stream of cars that were traveling half way down the dead end street before they turned around just before Baby's house. He knew they were the "Loon Crew." He wasn't sure what to do about it. As he looked down to send Baby another text, the Uncle came out of the house and drove away. Alan crossed the tree lined street and ducked into the patch of woods next to the small house. He made his way through the low growth and crossed into the backyard. He knocked on the back door and waited for Baby to open the door.

Chapter 9

Identity Theft

The Rainmaker whistled as he looked through the folders that held all of the information on what he called the "Lady files." He had transferred ownership of the 12 corporations into her daughter, Baby's name without a hitch. He marveled at how easy it was to do. With Lady gone, there was no one to watch over her daughter and at 18, her daughter wasn't wise enough to look out for herself. He had been sure to keep Lady's out of state address so that even if a Lawyer went looking for bank accounts they wouldn't think to search out of state. Lady was a local girl who never lived more than fifty miles away from where she was born. It made for a nice and tidy circle. When he had sent a mortgage modification letter to Lady eight weeks before she died, she had completed the paperwork and made it very easy for him to steal her identity again. He had been buying and selling her mortgage back and forth between her bank for the past eight years. Each time, he had his own phony mortgage company process her modification paperwork as if it were real. Each time she sent back the completed modification paperwork he was able to verify and update all of her personal and financial information. He had made sure that one of the merchants in town had hired her daughter so the last modification included Baby's information as well. Like all teenagers, Baby had jumped at the chance to work and she immediately wanted her own checking account. That made it easy for the Rainmaker to dump large quantities of cash into a secondary account that he had his bank buddy open in her daughter Baby's name. The Rainmaker had put a "hit" out on Lady. He thought she would never be allowed to collect any insurance money from the car accident he had staged on her two years ago. The local police, off duty detectives and Private Investigators for hire had surveilled her into the ground. Surveillance is legal on an open auto insurance case, the company would pay to be sure that the injured party wasn't lying about their injuries. Lady had injured her wrist in the accident and she would have received about eight thousand dollars if she had lived. He had done everything in his power and applied all of the tactics that his group had developed in what they called the "Face in the crowd scam," named for an old movie with a drunk who achieved fame and was driven into insanity. He had poured on the pressure and his plan worked, after nine months of relentless surveillance, Lady killed herself. All of her information and her daughters had been updated in the last modification packet where, right under her nose, he had included documents for Lady to sign that applied to updating the status of the corporate filings. Everything was fairly recent when she died so it was easy to organize new documents to file. In the business they were called "Muppets," borrowers who had no knowledge or capacity to know what they were signing. He had made sure to pay Baby enough money to be able to live on her own and one of his guys had introduced her to a real dirt bag boyfriend so that she would be compelled to move in with him. Typically, and the day before her Mother had killed herself, Baby had made an argument with her and moved out to live with the dirt bag boyfriend. He couldn't have planned it better. Now all he had to do was sit back and let things continue to run as they always did. If the Mayor knew how far he had gone to ruin his lovers life he might regret it so he never let on that he was involved. Besides, the Mayor had all that extra money to keep him company, he should be happy. The Rainmaker had the job of cleaning up the mess. He still had all his equipment at Lady's house recording sound and video twenty-four hours a day. Her computer had been hacked to verify all of her bank accounts and credit cards— she had almost nothing but he had to search everything. He packed up his folders and left the little Library office that he worked in whenever he was in town, and headed out to dinner with new friends. The Rainmaker was enjoying his dinner with two Artists who had just been placed in the Art House. The crowd was heavy as usual in the best eatery in Sicktowne and he was relieved to be able to relax. He was staring at his cell phone and going over the figures from the sales at the Art House. Sales were steadily increasing and he was diverting a lot of the money to a private account. Before her death, Lady had managed to find herself a tenacious Lawyer who would not stop pursuing the settlement from the "staged" car accident. The Rainmaker would have to pay it out of his own pocket because the insurance company information that was used at the scene was false. He had paid the driver one thousand dollars to slam her truck into the back of Lady's car. It was planned to precipitate the legal surveillance that drove Lady to her death. The relentless Lawyer was deeply involved with the oldest community group in town and he knew how these things went but he had just enrolled his second kid in college and he wanted money to pay for tuition. The Rainmaker thought about sending him a message but he knew that the Lawyer would more than likely complain to the Mayor since they were good friends. The Rainmaker also did not want to give away his identity and reveal his efforts in the scam. He also did not want to bring a war upon himself with the murderous community group that the Lawyer was past President of, over a one hundred thousand dollar payout. He put his phone away and decided to enjoy his food.

Chapter 10

In the family way

Mickey was driving home from seeing Baby. He
felt a sudden and overwhelming rise of emotion.
He pulled his car over to the side of the road and
stared out the window at Kingdom Lake. The lake
was being overgrown by grass as fertilizer from
the lawns of the surrounding houses ran off into it.
The tips of long strands of grass rippled up from
the bottom of the lake and created a surface lake of
grass that moved rhythmically in the breeze. He
was recovering from introducing himself to his
daughter and from spending time inside of the
dwelling of his oldest and most beloved friend,
Lady. He began to weep with despair, his mind
wracked with questions. How could he have let
that woman raise his child alone? How could he
have been so blind? How could he replace the
beautiful spirit of the woman in his life? He felt
alone and empty in a way that had been increasing

each year and was not eased by his recent marriage to a "girl" of eighteen years old. Spending time in Lady's house had forced him to recall a lifetime of memories, many of them prompted by the scent of her all over the house. He couldn't bear it any longer and the pain of her loss poured out of him in torrents of tears. He lingered by the lake for an hour or so and slowly composed himself enough to drive home to face the relentless effervescence of his bride. He was expected to have a child next year and he had welcomed the thought of a family; that was before the death of Lady. He felt like his youth had died with her. He went into her funeral service as a young man and came out as an old one. His bride was wonderful and fresh and new! He finally understood that he had to accept that his heart was just not in it anymore. And now he had a daughter, he had fulfilled that goal, even accidentally. He would have to talk to Emerald about how to go forward in his life with her. He would have to reveal the identity of his daughter and he would have to find a way to regain his focus for life. He resumed his drive homeward and took comfort in the ritual of the drive. Emerald was not home yet and he was soothed by the silence in the apartment. He sorted through the daily mail and was surprised by the quantity of advertisements. Ever since he had accepted the Advisor position in the Mayors organization, eight months ago, he had seen a drastic increase in the mail coming to his home. He had gotten used to the auto insurance medical bills that had flooded in after Emerald had suffered a slight concussion in a fender bender six months ago. He just didn't remember getting this much mail before he was married. He could hear Emerald coming in and he left the pile on the kitchen counter for her to deal with. "Hi Sweetie," he called out. "Hi," she answered as she came into the kitchen smelling like a new car. "At the dealership again this afternoon?" he asked as he kissed her cheek. He pushed her long hair behind her ear. "Yep! Was a good day," she responded. "Ready for some dinner? I've got some yummy beef tips from the market. Thought I'd serve them over egg noodles with a side salad and a nice red wine." "Wow," he said with a tone of surprise. "I could go for that! Serve it up. I'm going in to shower." "Good thing, you smell of stale cigarettes. Where were you today?" Emerald asked as she began to unpack the bag of groceries. "I had a really tough day, I had to talk to Baby about her Mothers will, I had to deal with the trashy boyfriend and I had to muddle through the paperwork that goes with death. Everything that I hate to do," he said plainly. She could hear the exhaustion in his voice. "Okay, sweetie, go wash off and relax. I'll get things together and call you for dinner." He gave her another kiss and pushed the hair behind her ear again. "You're a peach," he said as he left the room. She was warming up the steak tips and boiling the water for noodles as she glanced at the mail on the table. 'So much junk' she thought to herself. She never knew what a pain in the neck it was to manage the mail! She hated it and she quickly sorted out the monthly household bills and threw everything else into the trash. She kicked her shoes off in the living room and put the bills on Mickey's desk. She took a moment to enjoy the view from the large window overlooking the patio. She missed living in her family home. The apartment was beautiful but she wasn't used to living around so many people. She missed the privacy that came from sitting in her own back yard. It was impossible to barbeque or to sit quietly outside and every time she left she felt that people would be able to keep track of her schedule. She didn't know where these feelings were coming from but she had never had them before she moved into the Linen building. It seemed to increase after her car accident. She was noticing that every morning at 8:30 a.m the landline phone in the apartment would ring just one time. Like a "ping" that tagged the phone. She noticed the increase in mail after the accident. She noticed an increase in people in the parking garage each time she went to her car. She couldn't determine whether it had something to do with the position that her husband had accepted as Advisor to the Mayor or if it had something to do with the car accident. Her Dad had warned her of the scams that were attached to the auto accident "industry." Mickey came out and looked refreshed. She walked him back to the dining room table and pushed a glass of wine towards him. "I'll serve the food, just relax," she said as he sat down. She made up plates laden with hot noodles, beef and brown gravy and brought them to the table. She had two small salads ready, some crusty bread and some butter. She sat and they ate in silence. Mickey was grateful for the food. He decided to slowly introduce the topic of family. "Em, are you thinking about a baby at all?" he asked gently. "Not really hun," she answered. "I really don't feel that I'm ready for that responsibility now. I'm too young I think." He responded, "And I think I'm getting too old." She was surprised by his answer. She believed that he was getting too old also but she would never tell him. "So, we gotta think about it some more," she said. "Maybe it's not the way to go right now." He sighed loudly. "Well, I found out something today and I want to let you know too. I am the Father of Lady's daughter," he said quietly. Emerald was flabbergasted. She put down her fork and sat back in her chair to take a long look at Mickey. He reached over to take her hand. She answered, "You never knew? Not in all these years? Isn't she eighteen years old already?" Mickey shook his head back in forth. "I never knew and she is going to be nineteen next month." He replied. Emerald picked up her fork and starting moving her food around on her plate again. "How do you feel about it?" she asked. "I'm fine with it. I'm shocked but I'm good. I've known Lady all her life. And I just realized something else," he said slowly "she's just like me, pure Irish." "Is that so important to you

Mickey? I never knew." Emerald stated. "Well, it's a pleasant surprise," Mickey responded, "and a gift from the Universe I figure. Mom and Dad will be thrilled." "So you're all set then," Emerald quipped. "I want to talk to you about something too." Mickey was slowly eating his dinner, he had taken a few sips of his wine. "I want to travel a little bit this year," Emerald started, "I think it is important for me to see a little bit of the world before I am tied down with children. I think this will be a good year for it. All my friends will be abroad with their college classes and I can stay with them and get some experience in the world. I love you Mickey and I want to be a wife to you and a Mother to our children but I just feel that if I don't get some living under my belt I'll grow to resent you. I'll grow to hate you. I don't want to feel like a prisoner." She was crying over her plate and it surprised her that she had exposed her feelings so freely to Mickey. Mickey was sitting and looking at her. He saw the young girl that she was, he saw that she was struggling with her choices and he didn't want her to. He had discovered his own personal struggle today as well. He watched her put her chin down and begin to wring her hands in her lap. He moved towards her and knelt on one knee as he put his right hand on her left shoulder and his left hand on her right knee. He looked up into her down cast face and said, "Go Emerald, go! I know what you're feeling, I never got out of here. I would have been an entirely different man if I did. Go! Enjoy your world. You are the same age as my daughter for God's Sake, Go!" They stood up and he held her for a long time in silence. In those moments, Mickey knew that his one true love was and always would be Lady.

Chapter 11

The Mayor runs—away

Mickey was reading over the papers that his lawyer friend had given him. He was trying to understand how Lady could have been owner of so many Corporations. She had never said a word about it. He was also realizing that if he was able to track down all of her assets, they would belong to Baby. The last will and testament that she had left did not mention anything about the corporations or any money in any accounts, yet the credit reports showed that she had 7 bank accounts and multiple credit cards. He was finishing his eighth phone call when the woman on the other end of the phone told him that recently, Lady Jane Winslow had sold her share of the stock in her corporation to a person named Lady Jaden Winslow. "Could this be her daughter?" she asked. He almost shouted "Eureka!" Things were starting to make sense to him now. There was one name that kept coming up with all the phone calls, the name was a friend of the Mayor, a Trustee that everyone called "the Rainmaker." Mickey had seen enough of it in his practice and he knew that Lady was a victim of identity theft. He also discovered that after she died, the Rainmaker had tried to change everything from Lady's name to her daughter's name. The Rainmaker didn't know that Lady had given her daughter a different middle name than her own and that difference made it easy for Mickey to prosecute him. Mickey was surprised to find the Mayors name on some of the documents. He always thought that he loved Lady. He seemed to love the money more. Shortly after the prosecution of the Rainmaker, his administration began to crumble. One day, the Mayor resigned. He was forced to face his own trial, they could never pin anything on him but he left the town in a scandal. Emerald would send letters and pictures from Europe every week or so and Baby didn't get any of the corporations that were in her name but she did get all the money that was in false bank accounts. Close to five hundred thousand dollars in all. Mickey's Mother had invited Baby to come to live in the family compound, a huge three home tract of land in the West end of town. Alan was a distant memory as Baby blossomed under the care and guidance of her Grandmother. Mickey stayed alone and kept on living in the Linen Building. He finished his term as Advisor to the Mayor and continued on with his own Law practice in Sicktowne.

www.ingramcontent.com/pod-product-compliance
Lightning Source LLC
Chambersburg PA
CBHW021440170526
45164CB00001B/327